ESSENTIAL ELEMENTS
FOR JAZZ ENSEMBLE

A COMPREHENSIVE METHOD FOR JAZZ STYLE AND IMPROVISATION

By MIKE STEINEL

Managing Editor:
MICHAEL SWEENEY

WELCOME to the exciting world of jazz! This book will help you get started by introducing the important elements of jazz style and improvisation. You'll also learn basic jazz theory and some highlights of the history of jazz.

Play-along Tracks

The exercises and compositions in this book can be played by a full jazz ensemble, or individually with the available play-along tracks. Listening to good jazz players is an extremely helpful way to learn, and playing along with the accompaniment tracks is an excellent way to hear how jazz is played. The full band arrangements include "sample" improvised solos for study and reference. And remember… have fun playing jazz!

ABOUT THE AUTHOR

Mike Steinel is an internationally recognized jazz artist and educator. He has recorded with the Frank Mantooth Orchestra and the Chicago Jazz Quintet, and performed with a wide variety of jazz greats including Clark Terry, Jerry Bergonzi, Bill Evans, and Don Ellis. Since 1987, he has been a member of the jazz faculty at the University of North Texas where he teaches jazz improvisation and jazz pedagogy. He is the author of *Building A Jazz Vocabulary* (a jazz text) and numerous compositions for jazz ensemble.

The University of North Texas pioneered jazz education when it instituted the first jazz degree program in 1947. Its flagship ensemble, the One O'clock Lab Band has toured four continents and has been the recipient of four Grammy nominations. Throughout its history, UNT has produced a host of fine jazz talent. Alumni of the program can be found in all facets of jazz and commercial music.

PLAYBACK+
Speed • Pitch • Balance • Loop

To access audio visit:
www.halleonard.com/mylibrary

Student Activation Code
7028-5871-9908-3559

ISBN 978-0-7935-9629-4

HAL•LEONARD®

7777 W. Bluemound Rd. P.O. Box 13819 Milwaukee, WI 53213

JAZZ IS...

- AMERICAN MUSIC that originated at the beginning of the 20th century
- A BLEND of many influences:
    - African melodies, rhythms, and instruments
    - European melodies, harmonies, and instruments
    - Early American musical styles such as Blues, Work Songs, Spirituals and Hymns, Ragtime, and Marches
    - More Recent Styles such as Rock, Afro-Cuban, and other Latin styles
- HIGHLY RHYTHMIC MUSIC, having historical connections with movement and dance
- MOSTLY IMPROVISED — jazz musicians don't rely completely on written parts

THE JAZZ ENSEMBLE

- CAN VARY IN SIZE
    From Small Combos – usually three to nine pieces with individual instruments
    To Large Ensembles – made up of "sections" (brass, reeds, rhythm, and strings)
- EVERY PART IS IMPORTANT
    Unlike Concert Bands and Orchestras which may have many players on a part,
    Jazz Ensembles usually have one player on each part.
- HAS A RICH TRADITION
    The original "jazz" bands were marching bands that played for social events.
    Throughout the 20th century the instrumentation of jazz bands grew:
        Jelly Roll Morton's Band in 1926 had 7 pieces
        Duke Ellington's Band in 1942 had 17 pieces
        Stan Kenton's Neophonic Orchestra in 1955 had 23 players
    The standard instrumentation of the jazz band today is:
        4 trumpets, 4 trombones, 5 saxes, piano, guitar, bass, and drums

Traditional Set-up

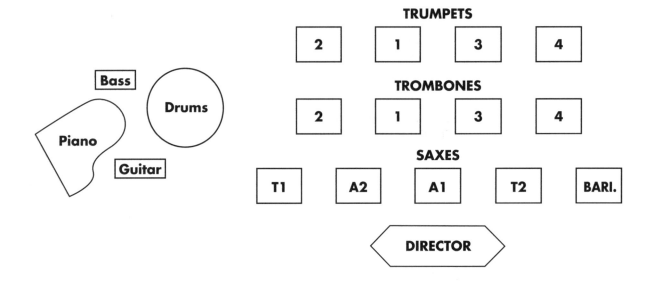

IMPROVISATION

- IMPROVISATION IS COMPOSING AND PERFORMING MUSIC AT THE SAME TIME
  - Jazz is usually improvised within the structure of a song or song-form
  - Music was improvised by the Greeks as early as 400 BC
  - Musicians of all cultures improvise to some degree

- IS JAZZ IMPROVISATION DIFFICULT?
  - Like learning a new language, it takes a little time but soon gets easier
  - The key: to start and not be afraid to make mistakes (a natural part of learning)
  - Everyone can learn to improvise with practice and help from a teacher

- HOW DO I START?
  - By listening to great jazz artists
  - By imitating the sounds you hear (and writing them down)
  - By developing good technique so you can play the sounds you hear in your head
  - By jumping in and giving it a try!

THE RHYTHM SECTION

All Jazz musicians need to understand the unique roles of the RHYTHM SECTION. Normally made up of piano, bass, guitar, and drums, it provides three of the basic elements of jazz performance:

- PULSE — steady time keeping
- HARMONY — playing the chords, providing harmonic accompaniment for melodies and improvisations
- RHYTHMIC INTERACTION — playing the rhythmic accompaniment for melodies and improvisations

Like a good conversation, jazz relies on interaction and communication.

All three elements are needed for jazz: Pulse, Harmony, and Rhythmic Interaction. But no one player in the rhythm section does all three jobs — they are divided among the players. If you map out the relationships, it would look like a triangle:

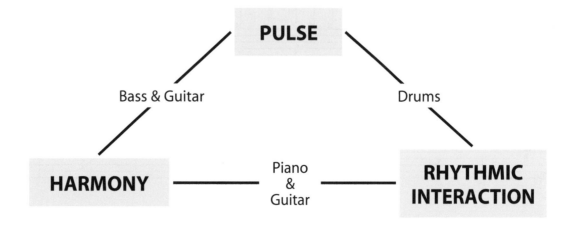

FOR DRUMS ONLY

THE BASICS OF JAZZ DRUMS

The Drum Set

Jazz drummers use a drum set that generally contains the following parts:

- Ride Cymbal
- Hi-Hat or Sock Cymbal
- Tom Tom(s)
- Crash Cymbal
- Snare Drum
- Bass Drum w/foot pedal

The Set-Up

The Drum Set should be set up so all the instruments can be reached comfortably. This will be different for each individual drummer. Here is an example of a typical set-up.

Reading a Drum Part

Drum set reading is different than other instruments. It is written on a five-line staff using a special clef sign or none at all. Notes with regular noteheads indicate drums (snare, bass, and toms) and notes with special "X" noteheads indicate cymbals. The hi-hat and bass drum will be played by the feet unless otherwise notated. Each instrument is assigned a particular lines as follows:

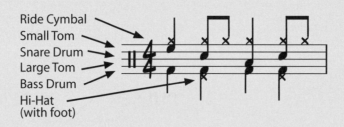

Other Special Notation

Drum Rolls

Cymbal Rolls

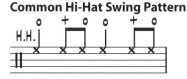

Special Hi-Hat Notation

Open Hi-Hat

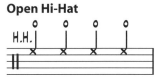

Indicated by "H.H." and a circle over each note. Played with hi-hat partially open.

Closed Hi-Hat

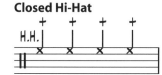

Indicated by "H.H." and a plus sign over each note. Played with hi-hat closed.

Common Hi-Hat Swing Pattern

Sounds like: Cheer Chick Cha Cheer Chick Cha

Proper hand position and grip

The proper grip of the stick is important in producing a good tone and developing an adequate sticking technique.

When using **Traditional Grip**, the left stick rests on the "V" between the thumb and index finger and on the second joint of the ring finger. The thumb, index finger, and middle finger wrap around the stick to hold it in place. The left hand remains in a "palm up" position and the stroke is made with a twisting motion of the wrist. It is important not to grip the stick too tightly.

The right hand grips the drum stick between the second knuckle of the index finger and the pad of the first joint of the thumb while the remaining fingers wrap around the stick. This allows the stick to bounce back after it strikes a drum or cymbal. This action draws the sound out of the instrument. Don't grip the stick too tightly as this will hinder tone production and speed.

In **Matched Grip**, the left hand mirrors the right hand grip described above.

Traditional Grip

Matched Grip

Both hands should hold the stick between one-third and one-half from the bottom.

Foot Technique in Jazz Drumming

The Bass Drum

There are two basic techniques: (1) the heel remains on the heel plate and the pedal is played with ankle motion and (2) the heel is elevated and the pedal is played with the ball of the foot. Experiment with each to find which is best for you.

The Hi-Hat

There are various techniques to playing the hi-hat but it is suggested that students begin with the "rocking" or "heel-toe" technique. In this method the foot rocks by bending at the ankle. The heel comes down on the heel plate on beats 1 and 3, and the ball of the foot comes down on the pedal on beats 2 and 4. This produces a crisp hi-hat "chick" on beats 2 and 4 and is a fundamental part of playing the basic swing pattern.

THE BASICS OF JAZZ STYLE

Attacks and Releases

In traditional music (Concert Band and Orchestra) you use a "Tah" articulation to begin a note and taper the note at the end.

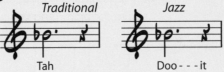

In jazz it is common to use a "Doo" attack (soft and legato) to begin a note. It is also common to end the note with the tongue. This "tongue-stop" gives the music a rhythmic feeling.

Note: *Although guitarists, pianists, bassists, and drummers do not articulate with the tongue (Tah, Doo, Bah, Dit, or Dot) the scat syllables on this page are meant as a guide to characteristic jazz articulation.*

1. ATTACKS AND RELEASES

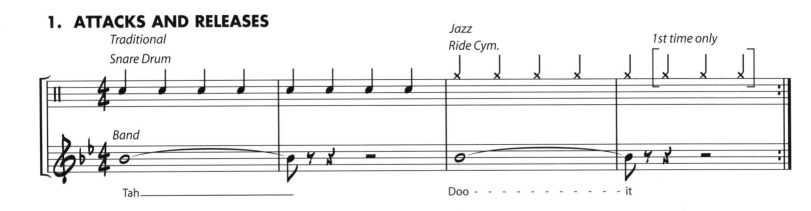

Accenting "2 and 4"

For most traditional music the important beats in 4/4 time are 1 and 3. In jazz, however, the emphasis is usually on beats 2 and 4. Emphasizing "2 and 4" gives the music a jazz feeling.

2. ACCENTING 2 AND 4

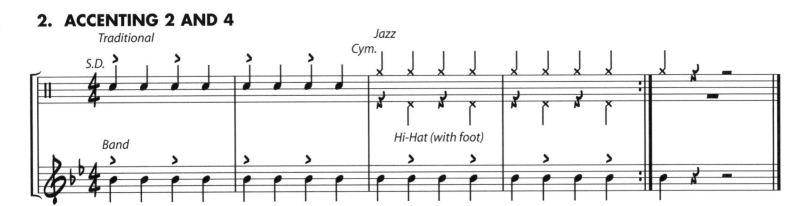

Note: *In jazz drumming, accents on 2 and 4 are achieved by adding the hi-hat and/or snare drum.*

Playing Doo and Bah (Full Value Notes)

In jazz, notes marked with a dash (tenuto) or an accent are played full value with a soft legato articulation. The scat (vocal) syllables "Doo" and "Bah" will help you hear the sound of these articulations. Remember in jazz it is important to play full value notes with a legato articulation.

Tenuto (full value) — Doo

Long Accent (full value, accented) — Bah

3. DOO AND BAH

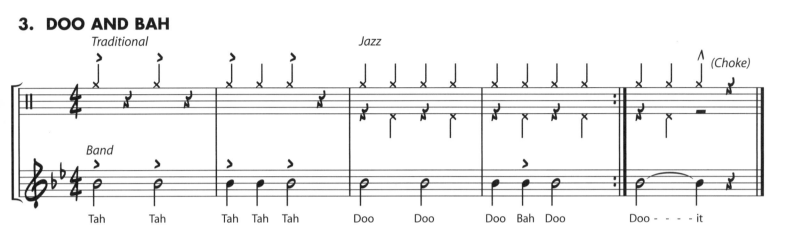

Playing Dit and Dot (Short or Detached Notes)

In jazz, notes marked with a staccato or a roof top accent are about half of full value. The scat syllables "Dit" and "Dot" will help you hear the sound of these articulations.

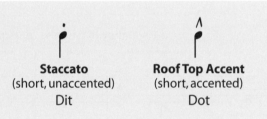

Staccato (short, unaccented) — Dit

Roof Top Accent (short, accented) — Dot

4. DIT AND DOT

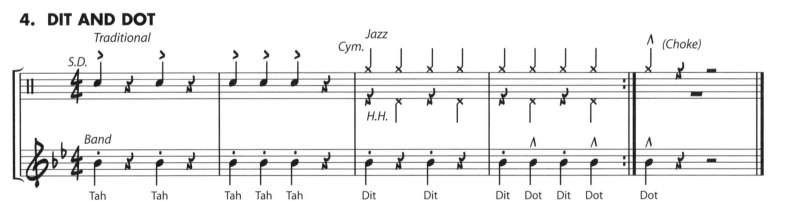

5. DOO, BAH, DIT, AND DOT

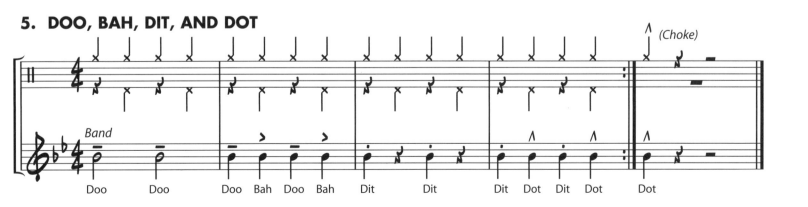

Swing 8th Notes Sound Different Than They Look

In swing, the 2nd 8th note of each beat is actually played like the last third of a triplet, and slightly accented. 8th notes in swing style are usually played legato.

6. SWING 8TH NOTES

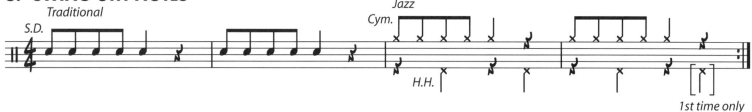

1st time only

Quarter Notes

Quarter notes in swing style are usually played detached (staccato) with accents on beats 2 and 4.

7. QUARTERS AND 8THS

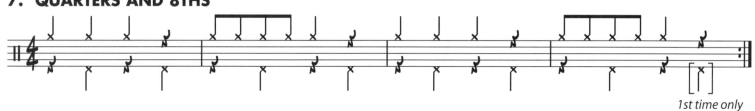

1st time only

8. MORE QUARTERS AND 8THS

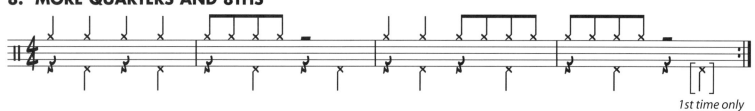

1st time only

Jazz Articulation Review

These are the four basic articulations in jazz and the related scat syllables for each.

Tenuto
(full value)
Doo

Staccato
(short, unaccented)
Dit

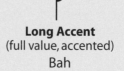

Long Accent
(full value, accented)
Bah

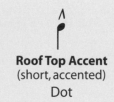

Roof Top Accent
(short, accented)
Dot

Quarter Notes

Quarter notes in swing style jazz are usually played staccato.

Swing 8th Notes

8th notes in swing style jazz are usually played legato.

FOR DRUMS ONLY

The Ride Cymbal

In jazz marked "swing" the ride cymbal reinforces the quarter note walking bass line provided by the bass player. These two instruments supply the rhythmic foundation of swing music.

The Basic Ride Cymbal Pattern

The ride cymbal pattern is usually played in a triplet feel, however it is not always strict. At slow tempos the pattern is very triplety but at faster tempos the eighth notes are played more evenly. In this book we will always notate the ride pattern in eighth notes.

The basic Ride Cymbal Pattern is notated as: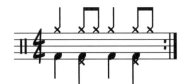

The basic Ride Cymbal Pattern sounds like: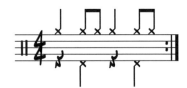

The Basic Swing Pattern – Playing "time"

This is the basic swing pattern for Jazz Drumming (with and without bass drum). Practice each until they are "automatic".

Achieving Variety of the Ride Pattern

Although many drum parts are notated with a strictly repetitive ride cymbal pattern, in practice jazz drummers use a wide variety of cymbal rhythms. Practice each of the rhythms below so that you can execute them with steady time and good feel. When playing the exercises and songs in this book feel free to use any of the rhythmic patterns listed below.

1. 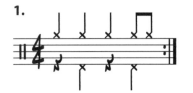 **2.** 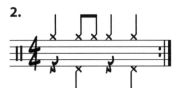 **3.** 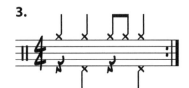 **4.**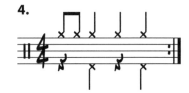

5. 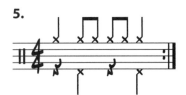 **6.** 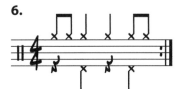 **7.** 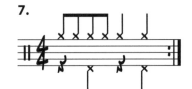 **8.**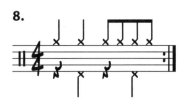

Using the Bass Drum in the Swing Pattern

When playing the basic swing pattern the bass drum can play quarter notes on all four beats of the bar very softly or it can be omitted. It is important to develop a very light bass drum as it can easily sound heavy and cover up the notes of the bass line. It is often said that the bass drum should be "felt but not heard".

9. SWINGIN' THE SCALE

10. MOVIN' AROUND

11. RUNNIN' AROUND

12. TRADIN' OFF

13. JA-DA

Bob Carleton

Syncopation in Jazz

When beats are played early (anticipated) or played late (delayed),
the music becomes syncopated. Syncopation makes the music sound "jazzy."

14. SYNCOPATING BY ANTICIPATING THE BEAT (PLAYING EARLY)

15. SYNCOPATING BY DELAYING THE BEAT (PLAYING LATE)

16. WHEN THE SAINTS GO MARCHING IN – Without Syncopation

James Black and Katherine Purvis

17. WHEN THE SAINTS GO MARCHING IN – With Syncopation

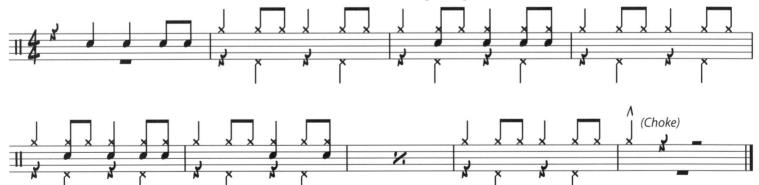

18. RHYTHM STUDY FOR JA-DA

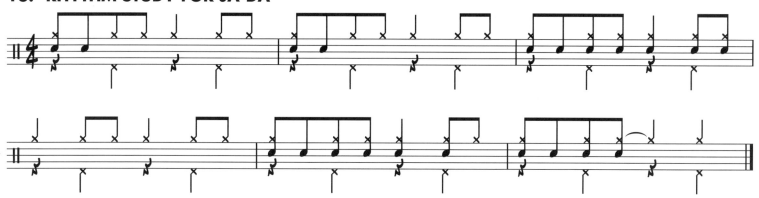

19. JA-DA – Full Band Arrangement – With Syncopation

Bob Carleton
Arr. by Mike Steinel

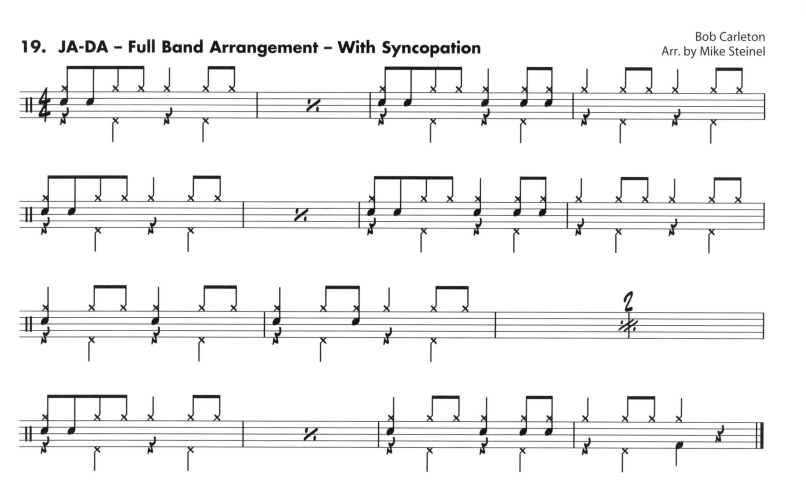

FOR DRUMS ONLY

The Importance of Coordination

As mentioned earlier, in jazz marked "swing" the ride cymbal and hi-hat (played by the left foot and right hand) provide the basic pulse while the snare drum, tom-toms, and bass drum (played by the left hand and right foot) are used to reinforce ensemble figures and provide rhythmic commentary for solos. It is important that jazz drummers develop coordination between the arms and legs so that reinforcing rhythms can be executed without disturbing the general pulse of the music. Exercises such as the ones below are an important part of the development of jazz drumming technique.

20. READING SWING RHYTHMS To play the correct rhythm with a good jazz feel, think (or feel) the basic 8th note pulse and the jazz syllables. You may simplify this exercise by playing only the snare drum or ride cym. part.

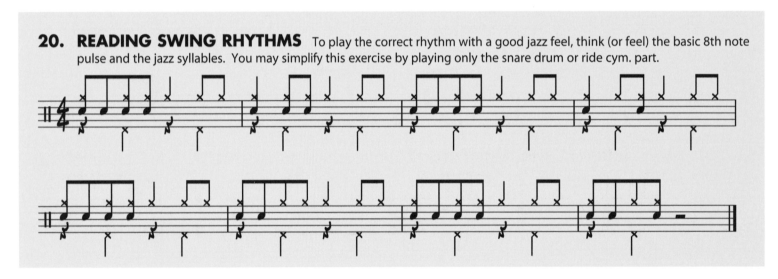

21. SWING RHYTHM WORKOUT #1 Try S.D. or Ride Cym. separately.

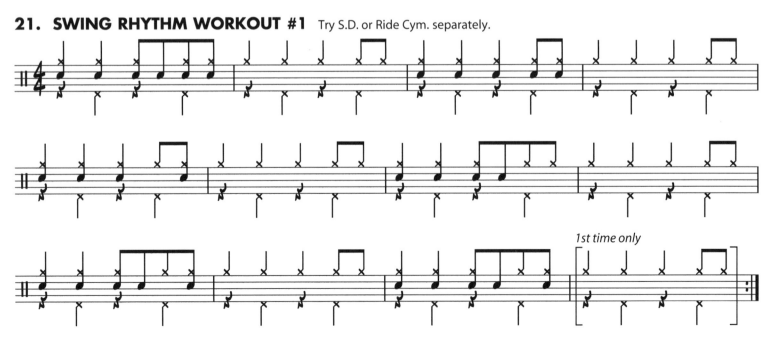

22. SWING RHYTHM WORKOUT #2 Try S.D. or Ride Cym. separately.

1st time only

23. SWING RHYTHM WORKOUT #3 Remember to keep the 8th note pulse going in your head.

Band

Dit Doo Bah   Doo   Bah   Doo Bah   Doo Dit   Bah

24. SWING RHYTHM REVIEW Try S.D. or Ride Cym. separately.

FOR DRUMS ONLY

What is "Comping"?

The term "Comping" is short for accompanying or accompaniment and is the term jazz musicians use to denote the harmonic and rhythmic support they provide for the jazz ensemble. You may be asked to "comp" chords or "comp" time. Basically "comping" is what the rhythm section does when it is not soloing.

Comping Rhythms

It is important that pianists, guitarists, and drummers use characteristic rhythms in their comping. Here are four common jazz comping rhythms and their variations. Practice these rhythms until they can be executed accurately with a good feeling of swing.

Four Great Comping Rhythms

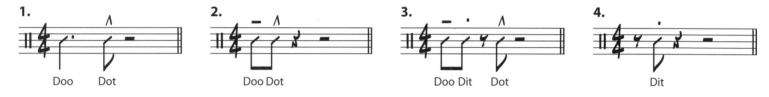

Four Great Comping Rhythms and Variations

Practice these rhythms first on the snare drum alone, then add a basic ride pattern using the ride cym. and hi-hat. When you can execute all the rhythms accurately while maintaining accurate and swinging time feel, go back and practice all of the rhythms on the bass drum. Work to maintain a dynamic balance between all parts of the drum set.

"Jazzin' Up" the Melody with Syncopation

Syncopation is the first step to improvising in a jazz style. Early jazz musicians syncopated all types of music, including marching band tunes, hymns, and blues songs. They called it raggin' the melody.

25. "JAZZIN' UP" A-TISKET A-TASKET

(Original Melody)

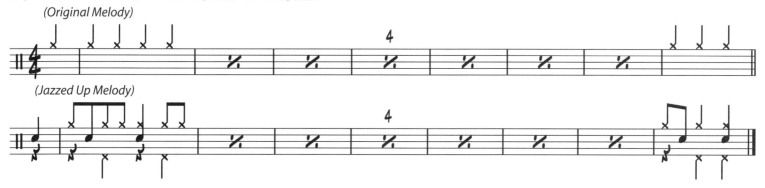

(Jazzed Up Melody)

"Jazzin' Up" the Melody by Adding Rhythms

Adding rhythms to a melody is another easy way to improvise in a jazz style. Start by filling out long notes with repeated 8th and quarter notes. Remember to swing the 8th notes (play legato and give the upbeats an accent).

26. "JAZZIN' UP" JINGLE BELLS

(Original Melody)

J. Pierpont

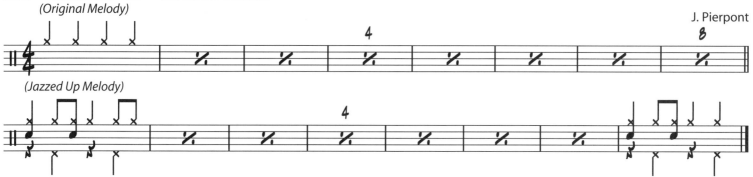

(Jazzed Up Melody)

MAKE UP YOUR OWN (IMPROVISE)

27. LONDON BRIDGE

(Original Melody)

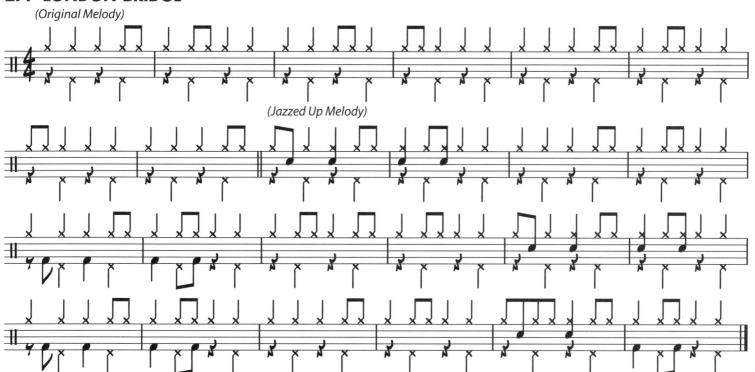

(Jazzed Up Melody)

Helpful Hint: Using The Melody Is Never Wrong

When starting to improvise, keep the melody in your mind. It is a helpful guide for beginning improvisers.

Swingin' With Jack

28. RHYTHM WORKOUT

29. MELODY WORKOUT Try S.D. or Ride Cym. separately.

Arr. by Mike Steinel

30. SWINGIN' WITH JACK – Full Band Arrangement

Note: Refer to page 22B for description of drum fills.

Style Review – Swing

• Use a soft "doo" attack rather than a "tah" attack
• Play quarter notes detached (staccato) unless otherwise marked
• Play notes followed by a rest staccato and accented
• Play 8th notes connected (legato) unless otherwise marked
• Play 8th notes with a triplet subdivision
• Accent 8th notes on the upbeats (the "and" of the beat)
• Accent quarter notes on beats "2" and "4"
• Use the scat syllables "doo", "bah", "dit", and "dot" to suggest the sound of each jazz articulation

Building Jazz Chords

Most jazz is harmonized with **Seventh Chords**. **Seventh Chords** are four-note chords built in thirds (every other note of a scale). A **Major Seventh Chord** uses the first, third, fifth, and seventh notes of a major scale.

31. *Sing or play on mallets*

Lowering the top note (called the seventh) of the **Major Seventh Chord** changes the chord to a **Dominant Seventh Chord**. Lowering the second (called the third) and top note (seventh) of a **Major Seventh Chord** changes the chord to a **Minor Seventh Chord**.

32.

Chords have specific labels called **Chord Symbols**. The first letter in a **Chord Symbol** always indicates the root or the bottom note of the chord. The letters and numbers on the right indicate the chord type (major or dominant for example).

Chord Name	Chord Symbol
B♭ Major Seventh	B♭MA7
B♭ Dominant Seventh	B♭7
B♭ Minor Seventh	B♭MI7

33. MAJOR SEVENTH CHORD WORKOUT (B♭MA7)

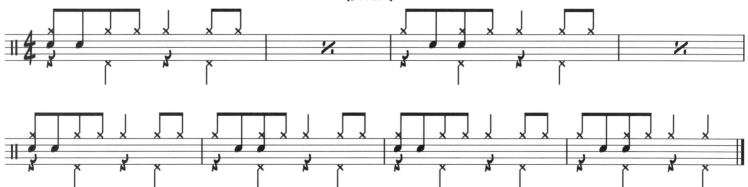

34. DOMINANT SEVENTH CHORD WORKOUT (B♭7)

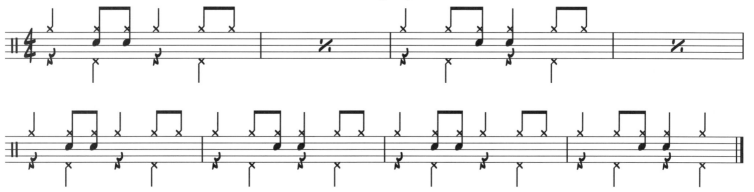

35. MINOR SEVENTH CHORD WORKOUT

The Dominant Seventh Chord is a "jazzy" chord

Because of its flattened seventh (often called a "blue note") the **Dominant Seventh Chord** has a very "jazzy" or "bluesy" sound.

The Blues Progression

The harmony of a jazz song is called the chord progression. The most common chord progression in jazz is the blues. Usually the blues is a twelve-bar repeated pattern using three **Dominant Seventh Chords**. The roots (bottom notes) of these three chords are usually the first, fourth, and fifth notes of the key of the blues.

36. LISTEN TO THE BLUES PROGRESSION – B♭ Concert

37. BLUES WORKOUT – Roots and Sevenths

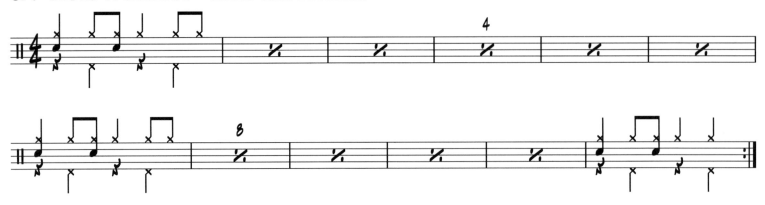

38. BLUES WORKOUT – Roots, Thirds, and Sevenths

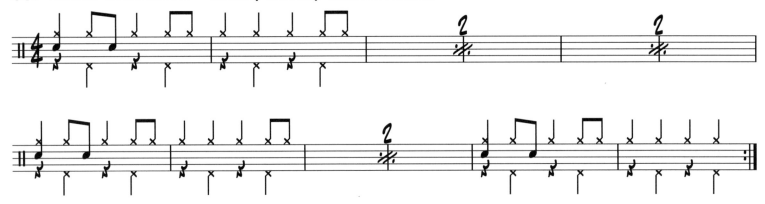

39. MAKE UP YOUR OWN – 2-Bar Solos using Roots, Thirds, and Sevenths

Building the Dominant Scale

You can build a "dominant scale" by inserting notes between the chord tones of the Dominant Seventh Chord.
This scale "fits" (sounds like) the Dominant Chord.

40. BLUES WORKOUT – Dominant Scale

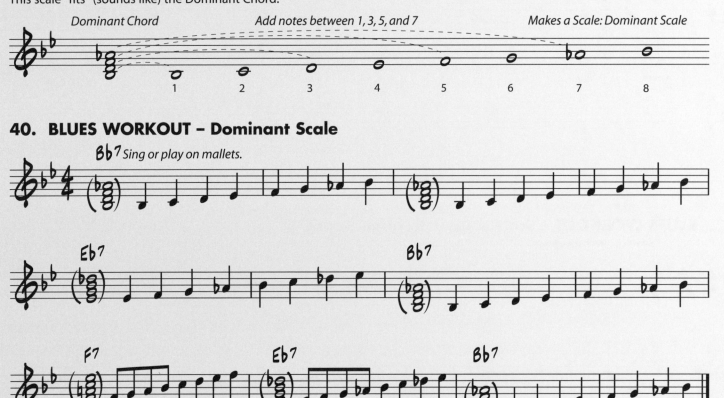

41. BLUES WORKOUT – Scale steps 1, 2, and 3

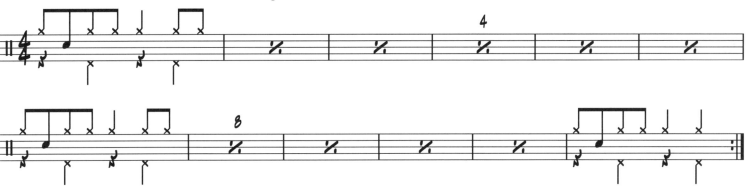

42. BLUES WORKOUT – Scale steps 1 through 5

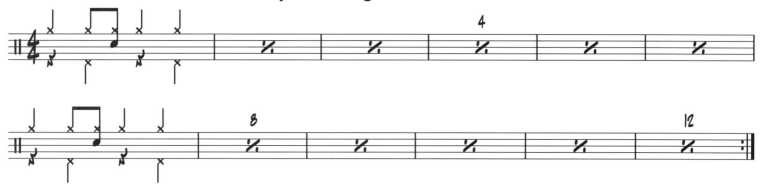

43. BLUES WORKOUT – Scale steps 1 through 5, and ♭7

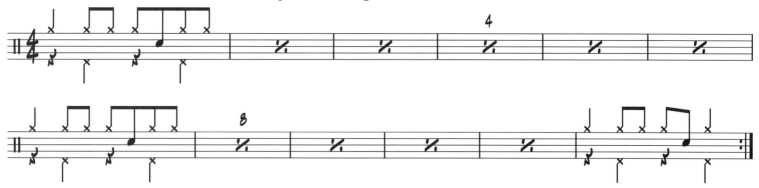

Helpful Hint: When you improvise, keep it simple. Don't try to play too many notes. Use occasional repeated notes and try to think of interesting rhythms.

44. MAKE UP YOUR OWN – 2-Bar Solos

PERFORMANCE SPOTLIGHT

45. OUR FIRST BLUES – Full Band Arrangement with Solos

Mike Steinel

FINE

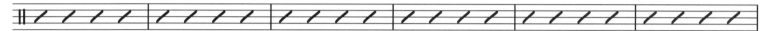

Solo Section: Improvise your own comping rhythms

D.C. AL FINE

St. Louis Blues (Composed by W.C. Handy)

46. RHYTHM WORKOUT

47. MELODY WORKOUT

W. C. Handy, often called "The Father Of The Blues," was a famous composer, bandleader, and music publisher. He was one of the first musicians to recognize the commercial potential of African/American folk music and he worked to incorporate these influences into the arrangements for his nine-piece orchestra.

Harmony Review

In Ex. 36 we learned about the blues progression in B♭ concert. Our version of St. Louis Blues uses a similar chord progression but in a different key: F.

48. LISTEN TO THE CHORDS FOR ST. LOUIS BLUES

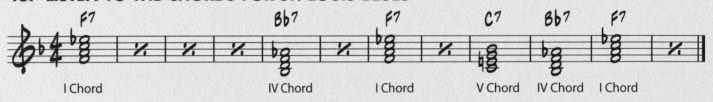

FOR DRUMS ONLY

Integrating the Snare and Bass Drum

Once you can accurately play the suggested figures in this book on the snare and bass drum while maintaining the ride pattern on the ride cymbal and hi-hat you can then begin to explore using the bass drum and snare (or tom-toms) together to play comping figures, fills, and solos. Here are some basic and common jazz figures that use the snare drum and bass drum. Like the comping figures earlier it is important that you practice these while keeping the basic swing pattern going in the ride cymbal and hi-hat. Keep the time steady and strive for a balanced level of sound from all the drums and cymbals of your drum set. To make the exercise easier to read, the basic rhythm of the figure is provided above each staff.

Suggested Practice Routine:

1. Practice the basic rhythm first (clap, play on snare, bass drum, an cymbals)
2. Practice the snare and bass drum parts separately.
3. Practice the snare and bass drum parts together.
4. Add the basic ride and hi-hat pattern.
5. Start very slowly (use a metronome) and then increase the tempo.
6. You may find it helpful to study each pattern and make a note of when the limbs play together and when they play separately. In the example below the dotted lines between notes indicate that those instruments are playing together:

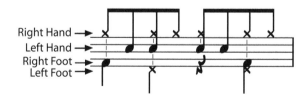

Right Hand →
Left Hand →
Right Foot →
Left Foot →

49. BLUES WORKOUT FOR ST. LOUIS BLUES – Roots, Thirds, and Sevenths

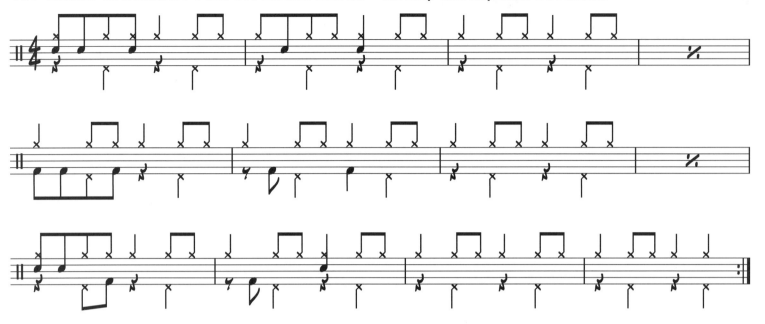

50. BLUES WORKOUT FOR ST. LOUIS BLUES – Scale steps 1 through 5, and ♭7

Improvisation Review

On page 9 we learned how to improvise by using syncopation (jazzin' up the melody) and by adding rhythms.
The melody to St. Louis Blues is already syncopated but we can add rhythms to make it "jazzier".

51. "JAZZIN' UP" ST. LOUIS BLUES – Adding Rhythms

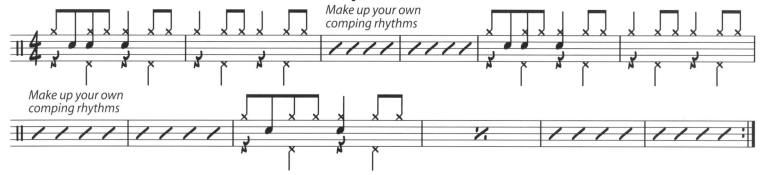

52. ST. LOUIS BLUES – Add Your Own Rhythms

Make up your own comping rhythms

Make up your own comping rhythms

Early Jazz

Jazz developed in the southern United States at the beginning of the 1900's. This new music, which wasn't even named "jazz" until 1917, borrowed elements from nearly all other styles of music: ragtime, European classical music, spirituals, hymns, work songs, field hollers, the blues, marching band music, and music from minstrel shows.

New Orleans was the center for jazz in the early years and New Orleans musicians such as Buddy Bolden, Joe "King" Oliver, Jelly Roll Morton, and Sidney Bechet were considered the finest performers of their time. "New Orleans Jazz" (or "Dixieland Jazz") focused on "group" improvisation with the trumpet, clarinetist, and trombonist often improvising at the same time over a steady accompaniment from a rhythm section made up of piano, banjo, drums, and occasionally bass.

After the first jazz recordings were made in 1917, the popularity of jazz grew rapidly. Jazz musicians traveled north to New York, Kansas City, and Chicago and then abroad. By the mid 1920's jazz was being performed throughout the world.

Louis Armstrong

Cornetist, Trumpeter, Vocalist

Louis "Satchmo" Armstrong (1900–1971) was born in New Orleans. Armstrong became famous playing with the bands of "King" Oliver and Fletcher Henderson before starting his own band in the mid 1920's. In addition to being a great trumpeter, he was a great singer as well and invented a style of singing using nonsense syllables which is known as "scat". He traveled the world many times in his long career and became the most famous jazz musician of his day.

Improvising on the Melody

Jazz musicians often improvise "on" or "around" the melody of a song. There are many ways to change a melody to create an improvisation.

53. ST. LOUIS BLUES – Original Melody

54. ST. LOUIS BLUES – Changing Rhythms

55. ST. LOUIS BLUES – Repeating Parts of the Melody

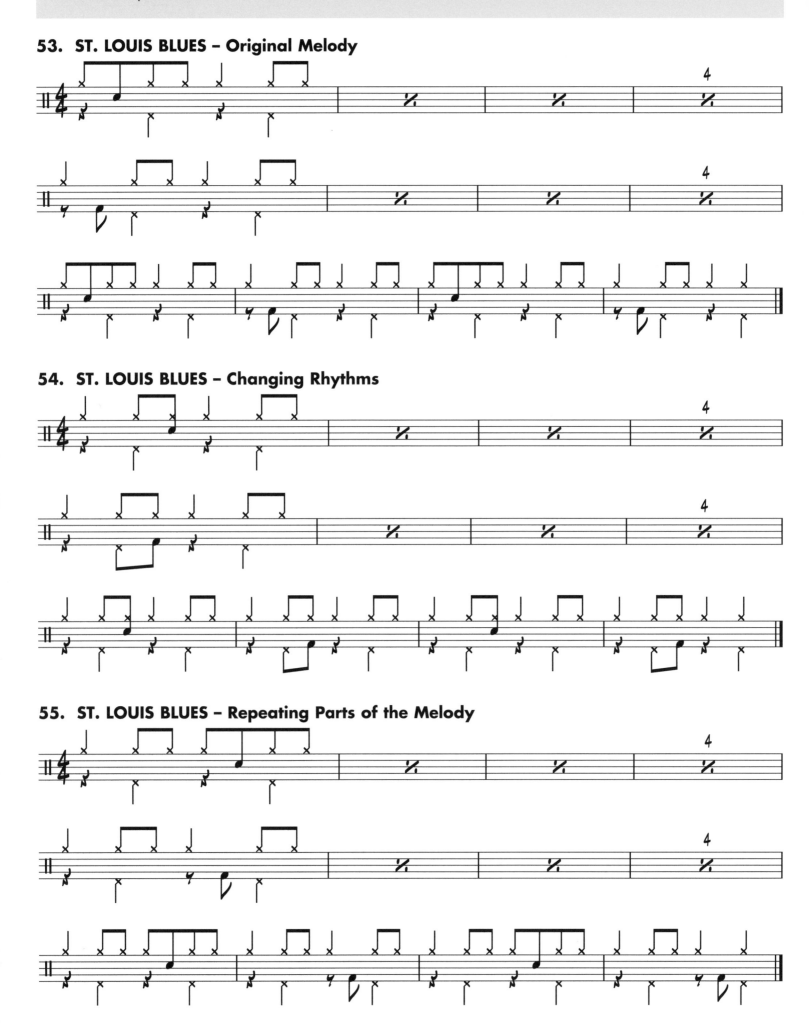

56. ST. LOUIS BLUES – Filling in the Skips

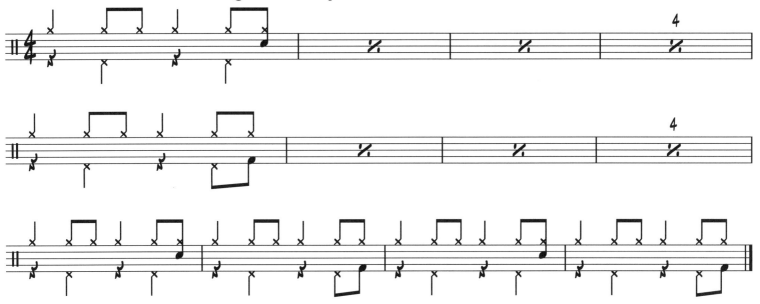

57. ST. LOUIS BLUES – Adding "Wrong" Notes (Chromatic Ornamentation)

A "wrong" or dissonant note (usually a half step off) can create a great jazz effect if it leads into a "good" melody note.

PERFORMANCE SPOTLIGHT

58. ST. LOUIS BLUES – Full Band Arrangement

W. C. Handy
Arr. by Mike Steinel

Note: On Ex. 59 the rhythm section may play the "solo section" from Ex. 58 (measures 19–30).

59. DEMONSTRATION SOLO FOR ST. LOUIS BLUES

Building the Blues Scale

The *Blues Scale* is a 6-note scale often used with the *Blues Progression.* Compare this scale with the major scale.
The lowered (or flatted) notes are called "blue" notes and should be played with a bluesy feeling.

60. *Sing or play on mallets.*

61. THE BLUES SCALE – With the Blues Progression

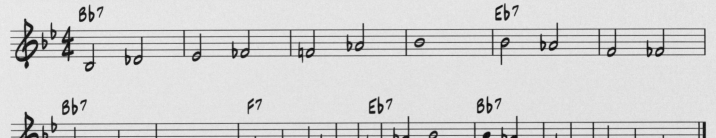

62. BLUES WORKOUT – Blues Scale (1, ♭3, and 4)

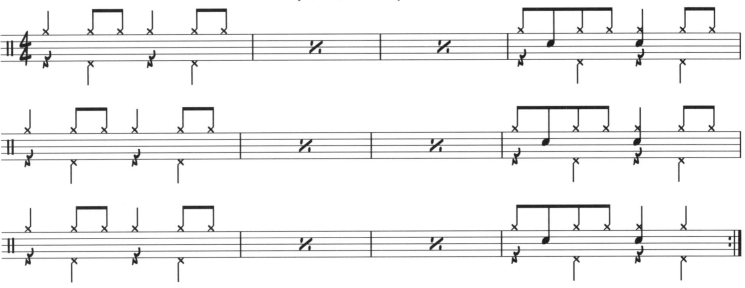

63. BLUES WORKOUT – Blues Scale (1, ♭3, 4, and ♭5)

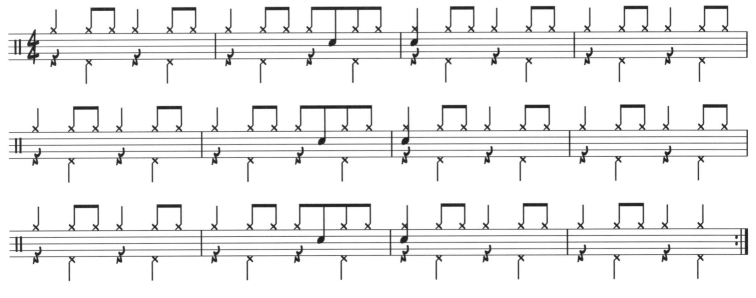

64. BLUES WORKOUT – Blues Scale (1, ♭3, 4, ♭5, 5, and ♭7)

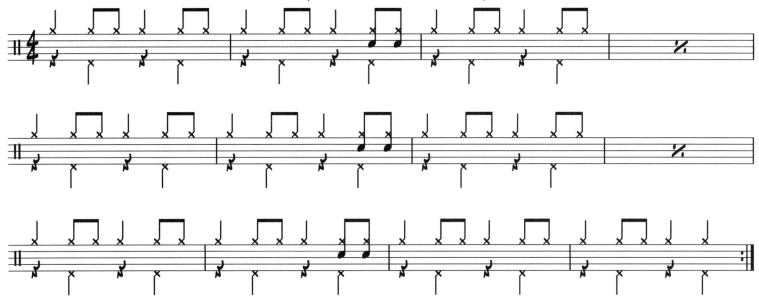

65. MAKE UP YOUR OWN – 2-Bar Solos

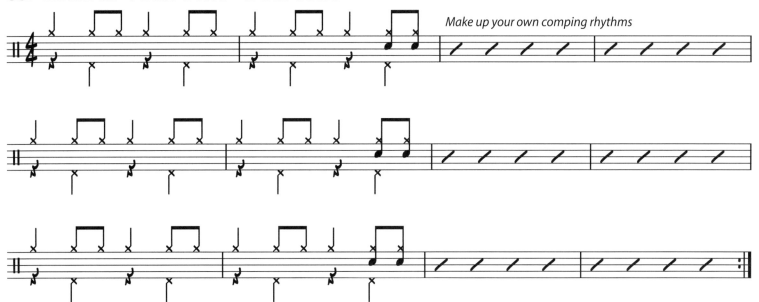

Make up your own comping rhythms

Riffs and Licks

Riffs and licks are short melodies that jazz musicians use when improvising. Riffs and licks often are built using the notes of the blues scales. In solos and songs they are often repeated two or three times. It is important that beginning improvisers memorize common riffs and licks.

66. RHYTHM WORKOUT #1   At first, try playing only S.D. and B.D.

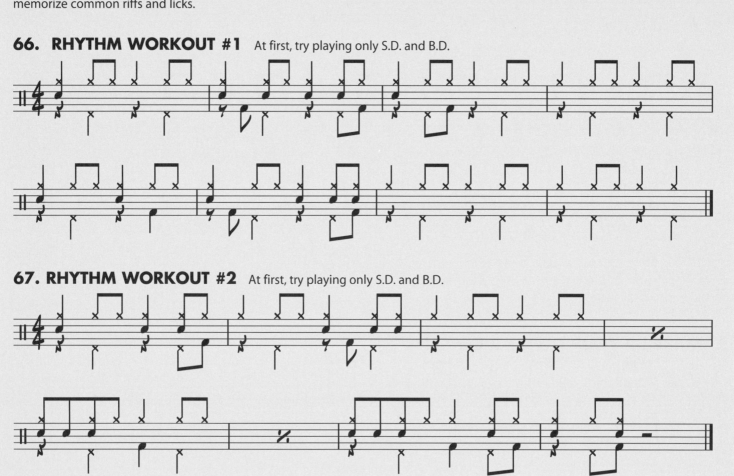

67. RHYTHM WORKOUT #2   At first, try playing only S.D. and B.D.

68.   COMMON RIFFS – Using Notes of the Blues Scale

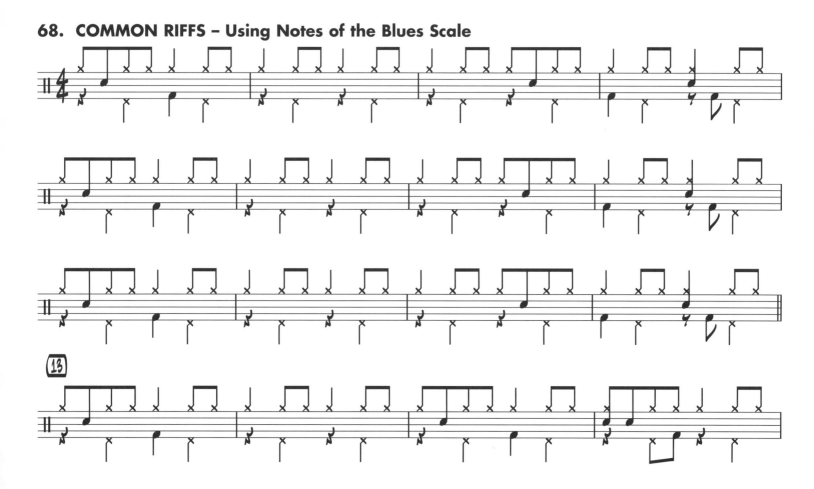

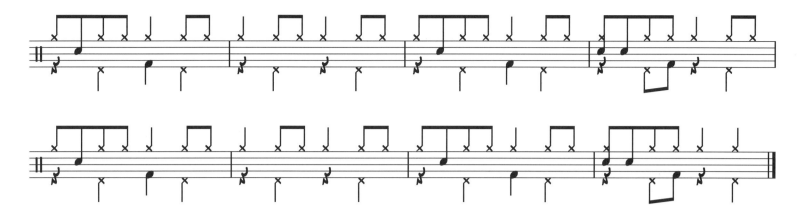

69. MORE COMMON RIFFS – Using Notes of the Blues Scale

70. THE MAJOR BLUES SCALE
This is another type of blues scale and is made up of the 1, 2, ♭3, 3, 5, and 6 of a major scale.

71. COMPARE THE BLUES SCALES

Jazz Expression – Bends and Scoops *(For Wind Instruments)*

72. THE BEND –
Start the note on pitch, lower it momentarily, then return to the original pitch.

73. THE SCOOP –
Slide into the note from below pitch.

74. MAKING THE BLUES SCALES SOUND "BLUESY" –
To sound authentic, certain notes of the blues scales are usually "scooped" or "bent". Bending and scooping these "blue notes" gives these scales a sad emotional quality.

The minor blues scale has three blue notes.

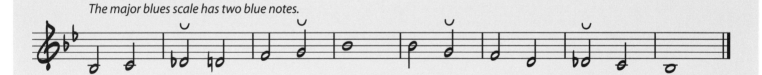

The major blues scale has two blue notes.

75. COMMON RIFFS – Using Notes of the Major Blues Scale

76. MORE COMMON RIFFS – Using Notes of the Major Blues Scale

Improvising with Questions and Answers (Call and Response)

Playing jazz is like having a conversation. The riffs and licks of a blues song or improvisation often sound like questions and answers. Usually, the "Question Riff" is played twice followed by a contrasting "Answer Riff" which is played one time. This "Question and Answer" way of playing music is called "Call and Response".

77. QUESTIONS AND ANSWERS

78. TRADING OFF – Questions and Answers

Make up your own comping rhythms

FOR DRUMS ONLY

Playing with the Ensemble (Playing Figures)

In jazz the drummer does more than just play the beat pattern of the song (often called "playing time"). Good jazz drummers usually adjust their playing to fit the melodies and rhythms that the ensemble plays. These melodies and rhythms are called figures.

There are two basic types of figures:
1. Ensemble figures played by the entire band
2. Section figures played by one section

Figures may be interpreted in a variety of ways. Ensemble figures can be reinforced with snare, bass drum, toms, and cymbals, while section figures are most often reinforced lightly while the ride cymbal and hi-hat continue to play the basic beat pattern of the music. It is important that the drum part enhance and not detract from the overall effect of the music.

What Do Figures Look Like?

Composers differ in how they notate ensemble and section figures.

The band plays:

The drum part looks like: — Slashes in the staff with smalll (cues) notes indicating the rhythm of the ensemble.

Or this: — The basic rhythm notated in slashes in the staff.

Or this: — The basic rhythm notated in drum notation.

How Are Figures Played (Interpreted)?

Figures such as the ones above can be played a number of ways. When learning a song it is best to play simple reinforcing rhythms in the snare drum. As you learn the figures better you can use more complicated rhythms and incorporate the tom-toms, bass drum, and cymbals.

The drum part looks like:

Can be played simply: — The basic rhythm is played by the snare while the ride cymbal and hi-hat play "time". This works good for "section" figures.

Can be more complex: — The basic rhythm is reinforced and enhanced by snare, toms, bass drum and crash cymbal. This works well for figures that are played by the entire band.

Note: *This is only a suggested interpretation.*

Figures Versus Swinging

It is important that drummers never let the playing of figures disturb the time and feel of the music.

FOR DRUMS ONLY

Playing Drum Fills

Drum Fills are short improvised drum solos that are:

1. used to "fill in" space after ensemble figures
2. used to "set-up" or prepare the listener for ensemble figures
3. used to mark off the main sections in a piece of music
4. used as solo breaks in a jazz arrangement

What Should You Play?

Drum Fills can be very simple or very complex. They can involve as few as one drum (good "swinging" rhythms on the snare drum can work well) or as many as all the drums and cymbals of your drum set. It is important that the fill you choose fit the style of the music and not disturb the tempo or the logical "flow" of the arrangement you are playing.

Here is an example of some simple fills used to "set-up" an ensemble figure and then "fill-in" or lead-in to the next section of the arrangement:

79. MAKE UP YOUR OWN ANSWER WITH THE BLUES SCALE

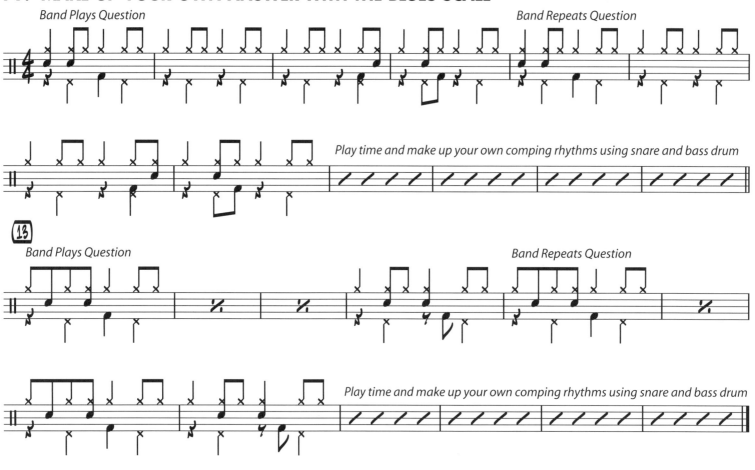

80. MAKE UP YOUR OWN QUESTION WITH THE MAJOR BLUES SCALE

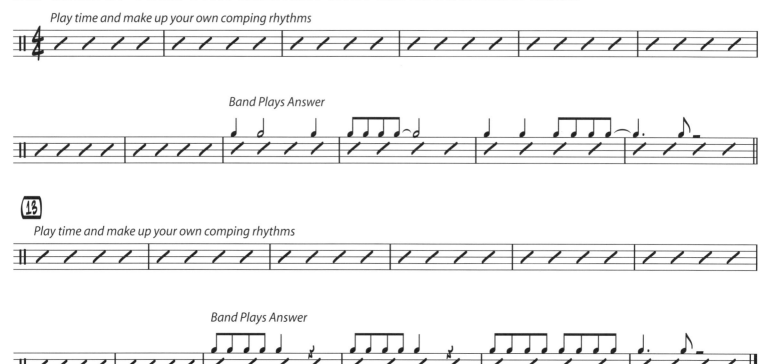

The Swing Era

In the 1930's and 40's, the orchestras of Duke Ellington, Count Basie, Benny Goodman, Glenn Miller, and Fletcher Henderson created a new type of dance music called swing. The strong beat and smooth "big band" sound made swing the most popular music of the time.

Duke Ellington

Edward Kennedy "Duke" Ellington (1899–1974) grew up in Washington, D.C. and led a band nearly all of his life. Although Duke was a gifted pianist, he is most remembered for his compositions and orchestrations. It is estimated that he wrote over one thousand works. Ellington is considered by many to be the most important jazz composer of the 20th century.

Count Basie

William "Count" Basie was born in Red Bank, New Jersey (1904), but his style of big band music is associated with Kansas City. In the early 1930's, Basie joined the Bennie Moten Orchestra, a "riff" styled band that specialized in playing the blues and performed primarily in the midwest. When Moten died in 1935 the "Count" took over the band, and under his leadership it became one of the most popular jazz bands of the era. Even after Basie's death in 1984, The Count Basie Orchestra continued to tour and please jazz audiences around the world.

PERFORMANCE SPOTLIGHT

81. "RIFFIN' AROUND" – Full Band Arrangement

Mike Steinel

Note: On Ex. 82 the rhythm section may play the "solo section" from Ex. 58 (measures 25–36).

82. DEMONSTRATION SOLO FOR "RIFFIN' AROUND"

Bebop

In the early 1940's, musicians began experimenting with a new kind of music which they called Bebop. Bebop was often much faster than swing music and its melodies and harmonies were much more complex. Swing bands played music primarily for dancing and focused on "ensemble" playing while the Bebop combos played for listening and emphasized improvisations.

83. RHYTHM WORKOUT

84. MELODY WORKOUT
Play time and reinforce the melody figures

ENS.

Theory Review – The Dominant Scale (The Mixolydian Mode)

On page 12 we learned that the dominant scale can be built by inserting notes between the tones of a dominant chord. The dominant scale is also known as the mixolydian mode ("mode" is another name for "scale").

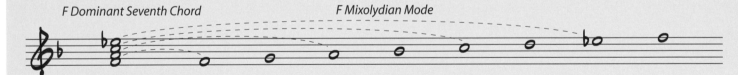

F Dominant Seventh Chord   *F Mixolydian Mode*

85. MIXOLYDIAN WORKOUT – Scale Steps 1–5

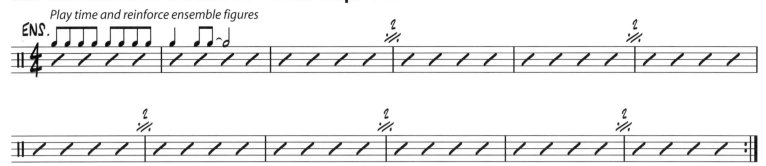

86. MIXOLYDIAN WORKOUT – Scale Steps 1–7

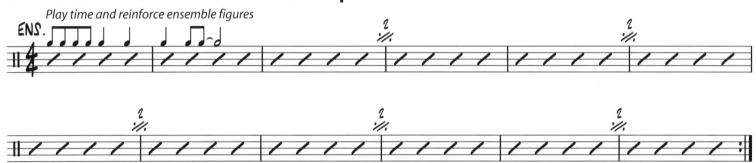

Bebop Uses "Wrong" Notes (Chromatic Ornamentation)

On page 16 you learned how you could improvise on a melody by adding "wrong notes" to the melody. You can also improvise on scales by adding "wrong" notes to the scales. Adding wrong notes is called chromatic ornamentation and bebop musicians in the forties made these "wrong notes" an important part of their improvised melodies.

87. "WRONG NOTES" CAN SOUND WRONG

88. "WRONG NOTES" CAN SOUND GOOD

Notes that don't belong to the scale can sound good if they lead into good notes (notes in the chord).

89. CHROMATIC WORKOUT – Filling in the Scale

90. CHROMATIC WORKOUT – Filling in the Scale with Triplets

91. CHROMATIC WORKOUT – Enclosing the Good Notes

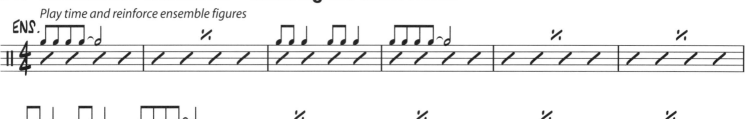

The Bebop Lick

The Bebop lick starts on a scale tone, moves by half steps down a step, and then returns to the original note. It is a very common Bebop melodic device.

92. CHROMATIC WORKOUT – Using the Bebop Lick

Play time and reinforce ensemble figures

 26A

Bebop Scale

On page 25 you learned how jazz musicians add "wrong notes" to scales. It is very common for improvisers to add a note between the seventh and root of the mixolydian mode to make a new scale called the Bebop Scale.

93. COMPARE THE MIXOLYDIAN MODE AND THE BEBOP SCALE

Bebop scales sound good with dominant chords because when they are played in 8th notes, the downbeats are always notes in the chord.

94. BEBOP SCALE WORKOUT – Running Down the Scale

Make up your own comping rhythms

95. BEBOP SCALE WORKOUT – Running Down from 3 to 7

Make up your own comping rhythms

96. BEBOP SCALE WORKOUT – Running Up from 5 and Ending on 7

Make up your own comping rhythms

97. BEBOP SCALE WORKOUT – Keeping the 8th Notes Going

Make up your own comping rhythms

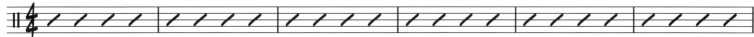

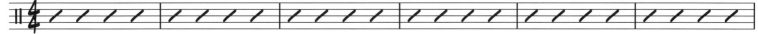

98. TRADING OFF WITH THE BEBOP SCALE

Make up your own comping rhythms

Charles Christopher Parker (1920–1955) who was known to jazz fans as "Bird" grew up in Kansas City. As a young boy he idolized Count Basie's star tenor saxophonist, Lester Young. "Bird" became a virtuoso performer on alto sax whose solos displayed fire, brilliance, and a keen understanding of the blues. Although he died before he received the recognition he deserved, his style became widely studied and imitated.

Charlie Parker

Dizzy Gillespie

John Birks Gillespie (1917–1993) was born in South Carolina. While touring with the Teddy Hill Band, he earned the name "Dizzy" because of his clowning and horseplay. His main influence was Roy Eldridge who was perhaps the most brilliant trumpet soloist of the swing era. In addition to being a great trumpeter, "Dizzy" was an entertaining showman. His puffed cheeks and bent horn made him a recognizable figure the world over.

PERFORMANCE SPOTLIGHT

99. "BOPPIN' AROUND" – Full Band Arrangement

Mike Steinel

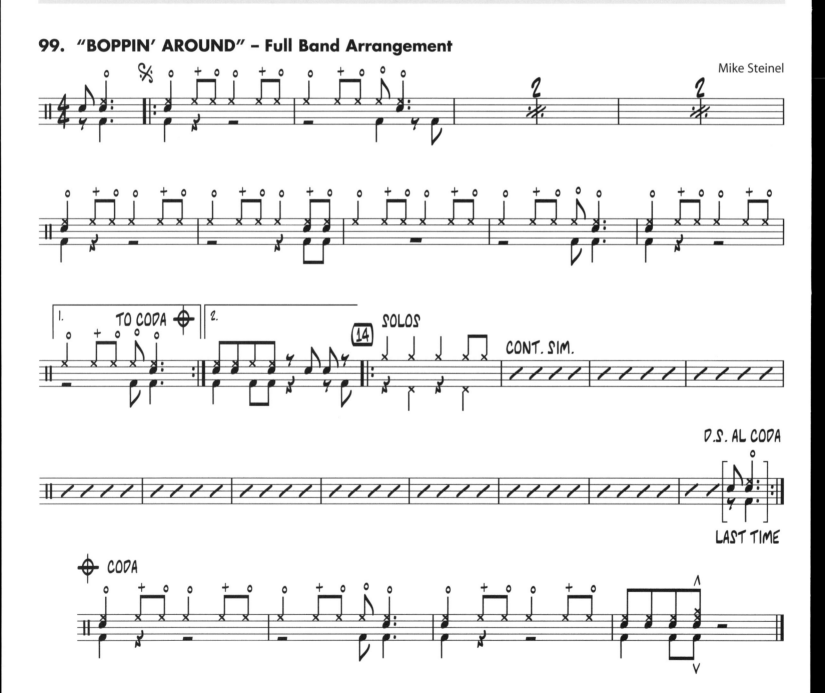

Note: On Ex. 100 the rhythm section may play the "solo section" from Ex. 99 (measures 14–25).

100. DEMONSTRATION SOLO FOR "BOPPIN' AROUND"

FOR DRUMS ONLY

Basic Beat Patterns

The modern jazz drummer is expected to know various styles of drum beats. Below are some basic drum beat patterns that should be mastered.

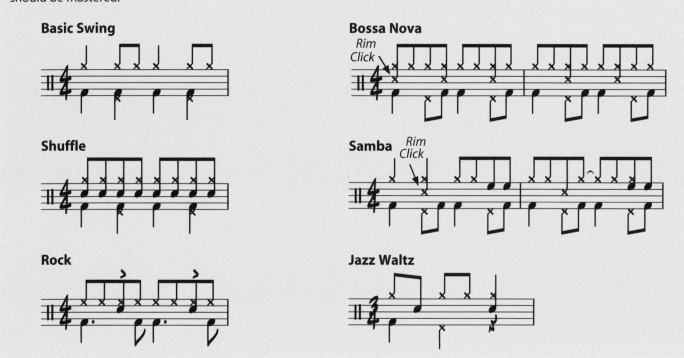

Latin and Rock Styles

Latin Jazz or Jazz Rock styles are played much differently than swing style. The 8th notes in Latin and Rock are played evenly, and articulations are often quite different than in swing style.

101. COMPARE THE 8TH NOTES

Swing Style (with triplet feel)   *Latin or Rock Style (with even 8th notes)*

102. QUARTER NOTES *In Latin and Rock these are often legato.*

Swing Style   *Latin or Rock Style*

103. 8TH NOTES *Often staccato or a combination of staccato and legato.*

Latin or Rock Style
Cym. dome or Cowbell

Swing Style

104. LATIN/ROCK RHYTHM WORKOUT #1 *This is a very basic Cha-Cha pattern.*

Cym. dome or Cowbell   *1st time only*

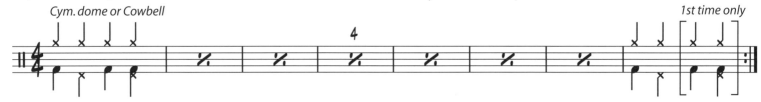

105. LATIN/ROCK RHYTHM WORKOUT #2 *This is a very basic Bossa Nova pattern.*

Ride Cym.   *1st time only*

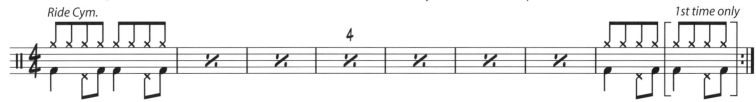

106. LATIN/ROCK RHYTHM WORKOUT #3 *Cha-Cha pattern.*

Cym. dome or Cowbell   *1st time only*

107. MAKE UP YOUR OWN *Bossa Nova pattern.*

Rock and Jazz: The Various Roles of the Drum Set

There are many fundamental differences in the way drums are played in rock music and jazz music.

In Rock Music

The bass drum and snare drum are the main time keepers and the drum set mainly supplies the pulse of the music.

In Jazz

The ride cymbal and the hi-hat are the main time keepers. The bass drum and snare drum are used to reinforce ensemble figures and supply rhythmic commentary to solos.

Salsa Caliente

108. RHYTHM WORKOUT

109. MELODY WORKOUT

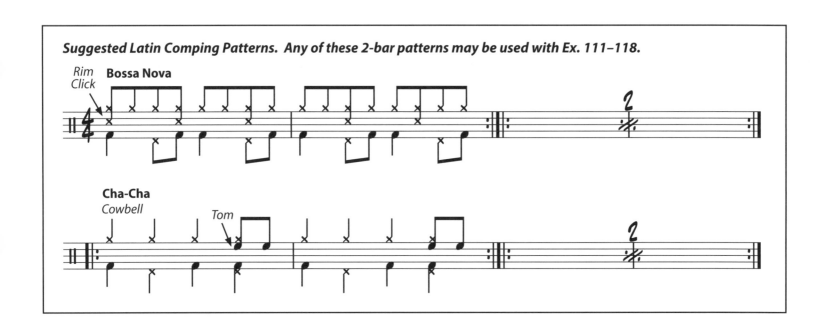

Suggested Latin Comping Patterns. Any of these 2-bar patterns may be used with Ex. 111–118.

Theory Review – The Minor Seventh Chord

On page 11 we learned that lowering the third and seventh of a Major Seventh Chord changes the chord to a Minor Seventh Chord.

110.

Building the Dorian Mode from the Minor Seventh Chord

Adding notes between the chord tones of the Minor Seventh Chord creates a new scale called the Dorian Mode.
The Dorian Mode "fits" or sounds like the Minor Seventh Chord.

111. DORIAN MODE WORKOUT – Scale Steps 1 to 5

112. DORIAN MODE WORKOUT – Scale Steps 1 to 8

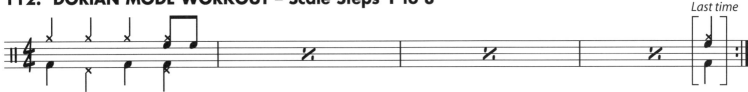

113. DORIAN MODE WORKOUT – Scale Steps 1 to 9

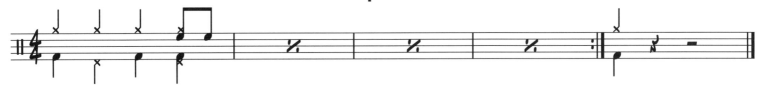

114. DORIAN MODE WORKOUT – Skipping notes and moving around

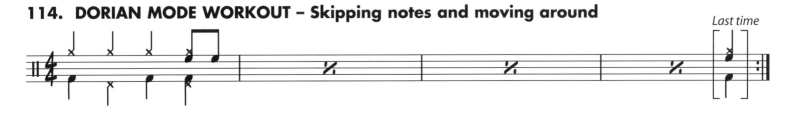

115. MAKE UP YOUR OWN – 2-Bar Solos Using the Dorian Mode

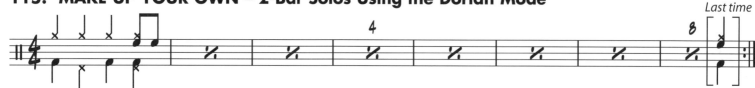

Blues Scale Review

The *Blues Scale* also sounds good with the Minor Seventh Chord and is common in Latin and Rock styles.

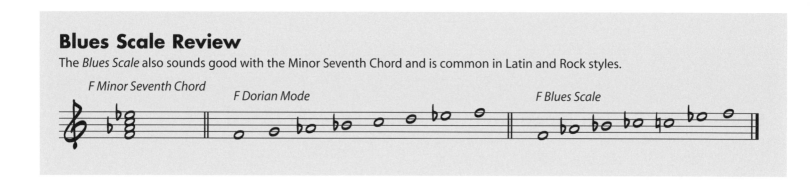

116. BLUES SCALE WORKOUT – 1, ♭3, 4, and ♭5

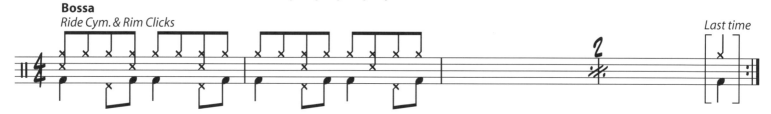

117. BLUES SCALE WORKOUT – 1, ♭3, 4, ♭5, 5, and ♭7

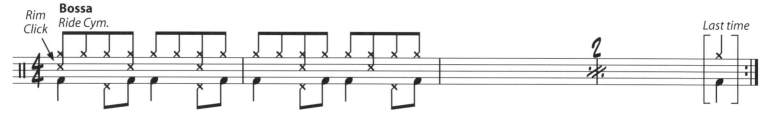

118. MAKE UP YOUR OWN – 2-Bar Solos Using the Blues Scale

Jazz Fusion

Miles Davis

The term **Jazz Fusion** is used to describe a type of jazz that combines non-jazz styles with jazz. In the 1950's, jazz musicians began experimenting by borrowing rhythms, forms, and instruments from many other types of music. Since that time jazz has been fused (or combined) with classical music, latin music, rock music, and Indian music, to name a few. **Jazz Fusion** often features a rhythmic style that uses even eighth notes.

In addition to playing bebop and swing, **Miles Davis** (1926–1991) was a pioneer of "Jazz Fusion" styles. He was truly one of the most innovative jazz musicians of the 20th century.

Miles began his career with the great bebop saxophonist Charlie Parker but quickly emerged as a leader who became and remained a trend setter for the rest of his career. He had a particular gift for finding and nurturing the most talented young musicians of the day. The list of musicians who played in his bands is a veritable who's who of modern jazz and includes John Coltrane, Cannonball Adderley, Herbie Hancock, Chick Corea, Tony Williams, Bill Evans, and John McLaughlin.

PERFORMANCE SPOTLIGHT

119. SALSA CALIENTE – Full Band Arrangement

On the accompaniment CD the solo section is played a total of 6 times. In performance, the solo section may be repeated as many times as needed.

Mike Steinel

Note: On Ex. 120 the rhythm section may play the "solo section" from Ex. 119 (measures 27–30).

120. DEMONSTRATION SOLO FOR SALSA CALIENTE

121. Jazz Ornamentation and Expression

In order for music to sound jazzy, it must be played with appropriate jazz expression. There are many ornaments and articulations which are peculiar to jazz and necessary to achieve a characteristic jazz feeling. These are some of the most common ornaments:

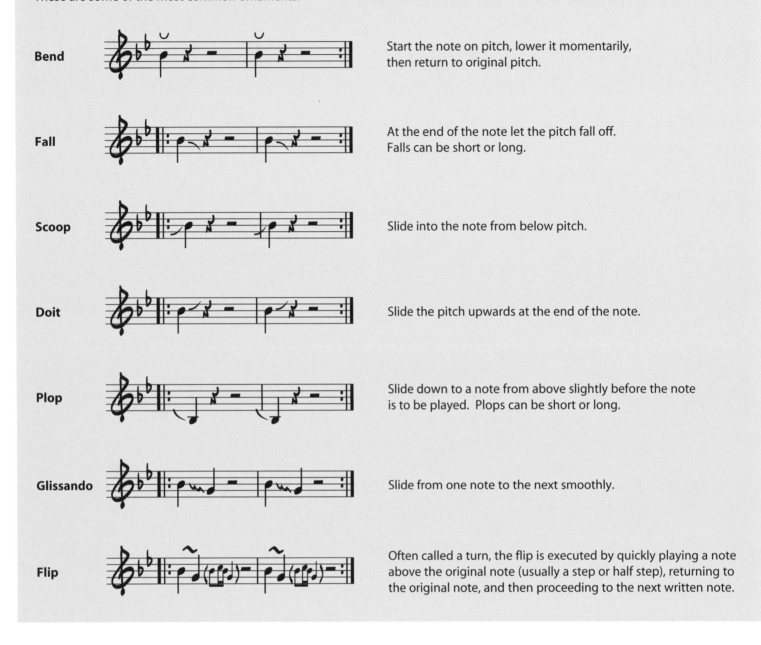

Bend — Start the note on pitch, lower it momentarily, then return to original pitch.

Fall — At the end of the note let the pitch fall off. Falls can be short or long.

Scoop — Slide into the note from below pitch.

Doit — Slide the pitch upwards at the end of the note.

Plop — Slide down to a note from above slightly before the note is to be played. Plops can be short or long.

Glissando — Slide from one note to the next smoothly.

Flip — Often called a turn, the flip is executed by quickly playing a note above the original note (usually a step or half step), returning to the original note, and then proceeding to the next written note.

Chord and Scale Review

Chord Type	Chord Symbol	Related Scale or Mode for Improvisation		
Major Seventh	B♭MA7	B♭ Major Scale		
Dominant Seventh	B♭7	B♭ Mixolydian Mode	Note: the Blues Scale can be used with Dominant Seventh Chords, Minor Seventh Chords, and the entire Blues Progression	B♭ Blues Scale
Minor Seventh	B♭MI7	B♭ Dorian Mode		B♭ Blues Scale